Lindsay Lepage

To Ronnie and Jane
—J.C.

For Uncle Sandy
—P.M.

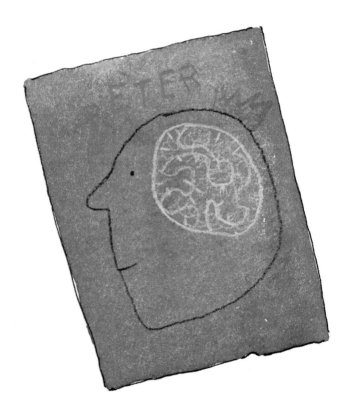

Library of Congress Cataloging-in-Publication Data
Cole, Joanna.   Your insides / by Joanna Cole ; illustrated by Paul Meisel.   p.   cm.   Summary: Examines the different parts of the body and how they work, including the muscles, digestive organs, and lungs.   1. Body, Human—Juvenile literature.   2. Human physiology—Juvenile literature.   [1. Body, Human.   2. Human physiology.]   I. Meisel, Paul, ill.   II. Title. QP37.C64   1992   612—dc20   91-61236   CIP   AC   ISBN 0-399-22123-9

B C D E F G H I J

Your Insides

By JOANNA COLE • Illustrated by PAUL MEISEL

Putnam & Grosset • New York

What's Inside?

Look in the mirror. You see yourself—on the *outside*. But have you ever wondered what's *inside* your body?

Bones and More Bones

Feel your elbow. Feel your knee. Do you feel something hard in there? Those are bones.

You have many, many bones inside your body—more than two hundred of them! They all fit together to make your skeleton.

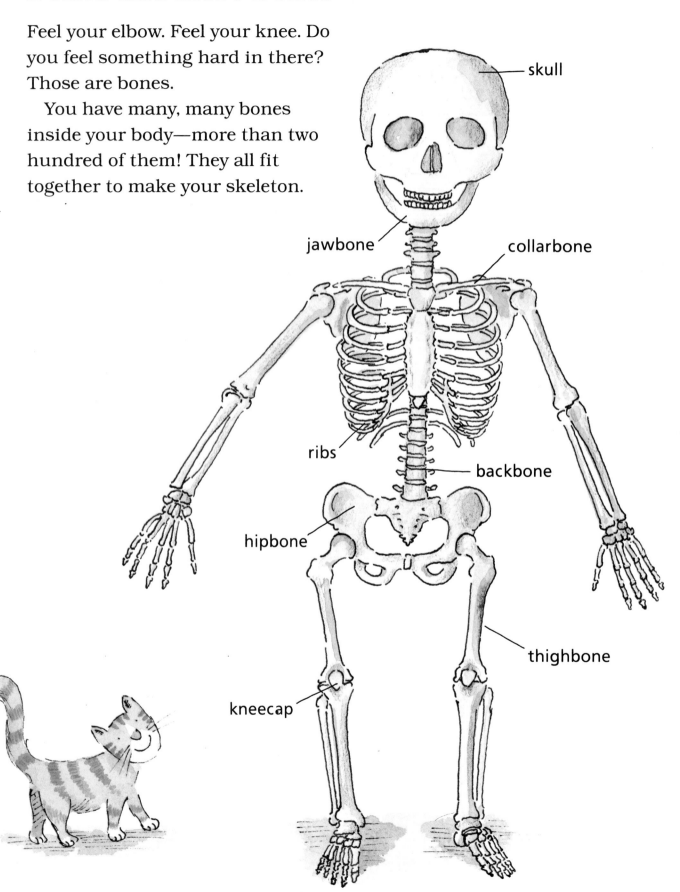

skull

jawbone

collarbone

ribs

backbone

hipbone

thighbone

kneecap

Bones Hold You Up

Your skeleton is like the frame of a house. Without a frame, a house would fall down. Without bones, you couldn't stand up!

Feel your bones
Tap your head. Can you feel your hard skull?

Feel the front part of your lower leg. That's your shinbone.

How many other bones can you feel?

Joints Let You Bend

Bones cannot bend—they are stiff and hard. But every time you move, you have to bend. You can move because your skeleton has joints. Joints are the places where your bones meet. Joints let you walk and run and skip and hop.

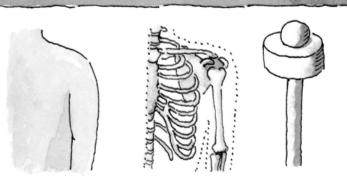

Your shoulder is a **ball-and-socket** joint. It lets your arm swing around.

Your knee is a **hinge** joint.
It acts like the hinge on a door
to let your lower leg move
back and forth.

Count your joints
How many hinge joints
are in one finger?
Can you count them?

Muscles Help You Move

When you feel the squishy part of your thigh, your calf, or your arm, you are feeling your muscles.

Muscles pull on your bones to make them move. Muscles are attached to bones with tough, stretchy bands.

Make a fist and lift it toward your shoulder. Can you feel your arm muscle getting harder? It is getting thicker and shorter so it can pull your arm bone up.

Muscles pull on bones

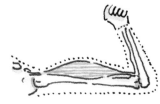

When a muscle is at work, it is short and hard.

When a muscle is resting, it is long and soft.

Think of all the moving you do every day. Hundreds of different muscles are helping you move by pulling your bones this way and that!

Your Stomach Mashes Food

Do you know where your stomach is? Point to a spot a few inches *above* your belly button. Now move your hand a little to the left. Do you feel your rib bones? That is where your stomach is—partly behind your ribs.

Food goes from your mouth down a long tube to your stomach. Your stomach is a bag that holds your food.

Your stomach walls are made of muscle. They churn and mix the food with stomach acid. Soon your food looks like thick pea soup—a soup with bits of food in it so tiny you cannot even see them!

Teeth cut and grind your food.

Food is pushed down a **tube** to your stomach.

Your **stomach** mixes your food.

Your Intestines Are a Long, Long Tube

Put your hand just *below* your belly button. What do you think is inside? It is a long, long tube much taller than you are! This tube is your intestines. It can fit inside you because it is all curled up—not stretched out straight.

The mashed-up food from your stomach goes into your intestines. Here the food is broken down into even smaller parts than before.

Your body uses the good, nourishing part of the food. The part of the food your body cannot use is waste. That passes into the lower part of the tube and comes out when you use the toilet.

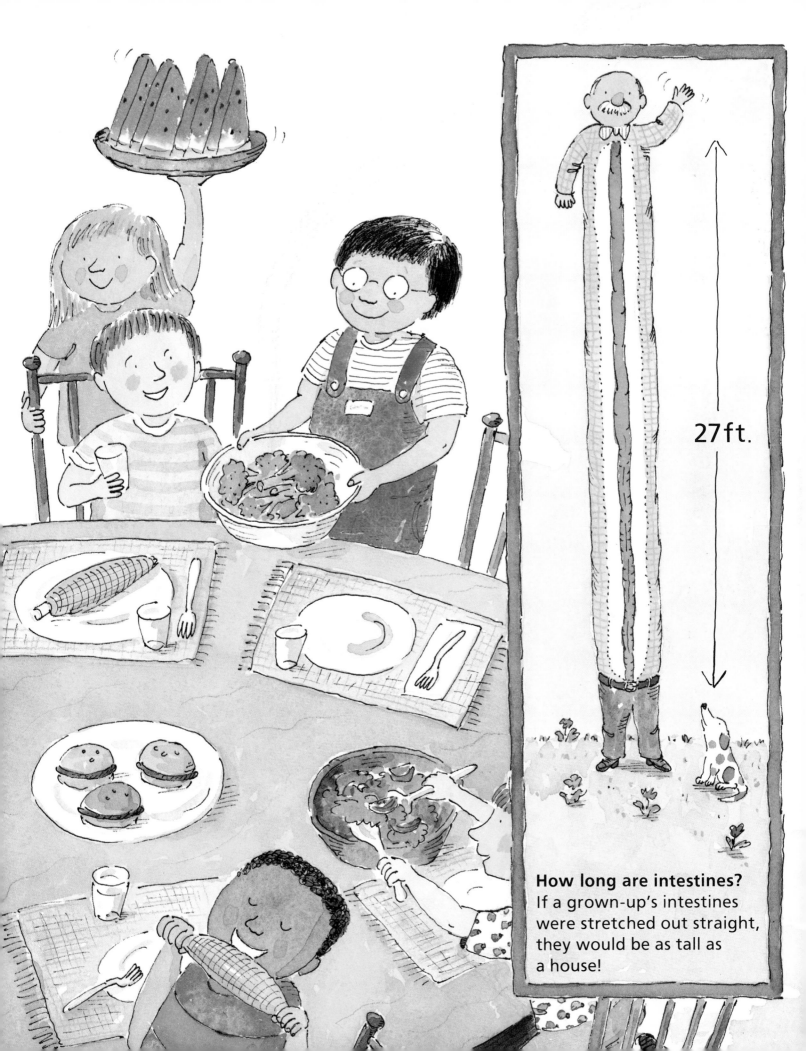

27ft.

How long are intestines?
If a grown-up's intestines were stretched out straight, they would be as tall as a house!

Your Lungs Take in Air

Everybody needs to breathe. Each time you take a breath, your lungs fill up with air like two balloons. Your lungs are like spongy pink bags inside your chest.

There is an invisible gas called oxygen in the air. We all need oxygen to stay alive. When you breathe in, your body gets oxygen from the air. When you breathe out, you get rid of other gases that your body does not need.

Air goes into your nose or mouth…

down your windpipe…

and into your lungs.

You can see your chest get bigger when you breathe air in.

You can see it get smaller when you breathe air out.

On a cold day, you can make a cloud There is water in the air that you breathe out. Usually you cannot see the water—the drops are too tiny.

But in the winter, the cold makes the water drops bigger. Then your breath looks like a little cloud!

Your Heart Is a Pump

Put your ear on your friend's chest. Can you hear *"lub **dub**, lub **dub**"?* That is the sound of the heart pumping. Let your friend listen to your heart, too.

Your heart is a very strong muscle inside your chest. It pumps all the time. It never stops—not even when you are asleep!

Why does your heart pump? The pumping pushes blood all around your body.

hollow spaces

outside of heart

inside of heart

Your heart works like a squeeze pump
Blood flows into hollow
spaces in your heart.
Then your heart muscle
squeezes and pumps
the blood out.

Lots of Blood

When you get a cut, you see drops of red blood. There is a lot of blood inside you. A grown-up has about five quarts of blood. You have about two quarts—enough to fill a big soda bottle.

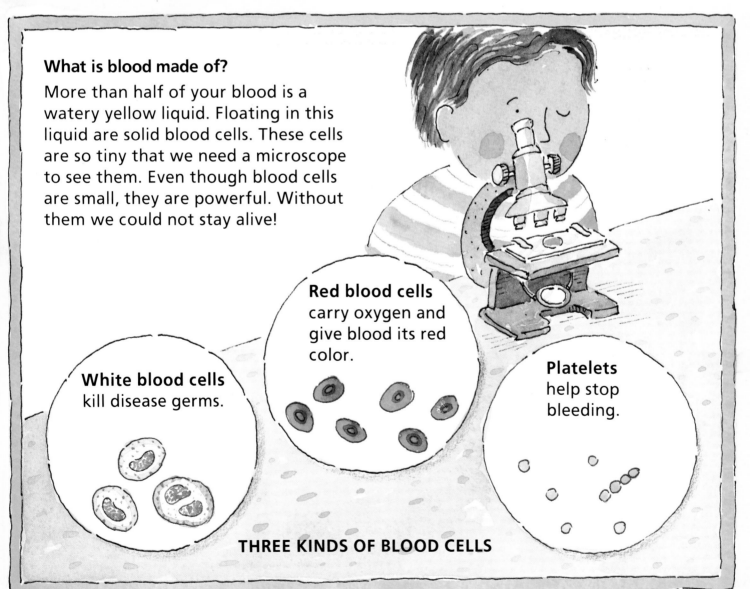

What is blood made of?

More than half of your blood is a watery yellow liquid. Floating in this liquid are solid blood cells. These cells are so tiny that we need a microscope to see them. Even though blood cells are small, they are powerful. Without them we could not stay alive!

Red blood cells carry oxygen and give blood its red color.

Platelets help stop bleeding.

White blood cells kill disease germs.

THREE KINDS OF BLOOD CELLS

Your Blood Is Always Moving

Blood keeps going round and round your body—over and over and over again.

Your blood flows through special tubes inside your body. These tubes are called blood vessels.

Blood vessels called arteries lead away from your heart. They connect to smaller and smaller arteries that carry blood all through your body. Blood flows back to your heart through another set of blood vessels called veins.

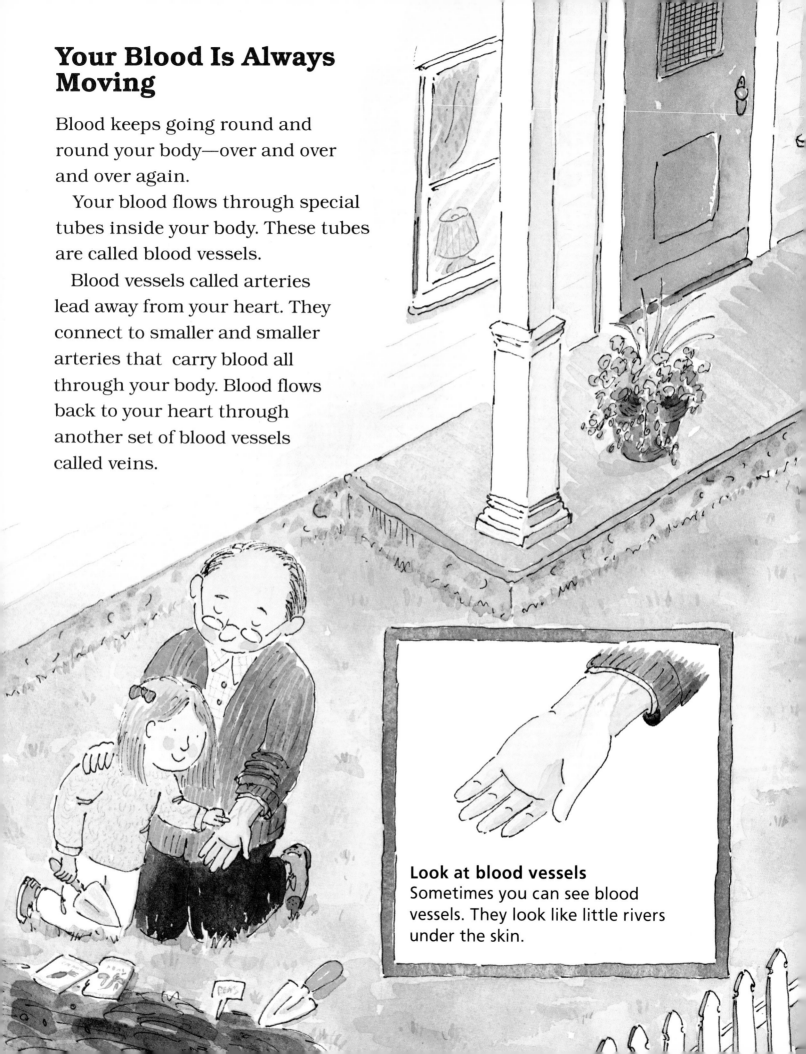

Look at blood vessels
Sometimes you can see blood vessels. They look like little rivers under the skin.

Your Blood Is a Delivery Service

Why does your blood have to keep moving all the time? Because it is making deliveries, bringing supplies to every part of your body.

Your blood picks up tiny, tiny bits of food from your intestines. It picks up oxygen from your lungs. Then it carries this food and oxygen to other parts of your body. Blood also carries away waste materials that your body cannot use.

arteries   veins

Your Wonderful Brain

Inside your head, protected from harm by your hard skull, is your wonderful brain. It doesn't look like much—just a pinkish-gray blob. But you could say your brain is your most important part.

You couldn't think without your brain. You couldn't talk without it. You couldn't even understand these words without it. Your brain makes you smart! But that's not all it does. Your brain is the boss of your whole body.

cerebrum

cerebellum

brain stem

Animal Skulls

RACCOON

Your Brain Is Your Control Center

Your brain tells each part of your body what to do. Different parts of your brain control different parts of your body. One part of your brain is in charge of your breathing and keeps your heart beating. Another part makes your muscles move. There's even a part that helps you keep your balance. How does your brain do all this? It sends millions and millions of messages through pathways called nerves.

Nerves Send Messages

Nerves are like telephone wires. They carry messages back and forth between your brain and your body.

When you want to move your arm, your brain sends a message to the nerves that make your arm muscles work. If something tickles your foot, the nerves in your skin send a message to your brain, so you can feel the tickle.

brain

spinal cord
(fits inside
your backbone)

nerves

Where Are Your Nerves?

There are nerves running all
through your body. A thick bundle
of nerves goes from your brain to
a spot just below your waist. This
bundle is your spinal cord. It
connects your brain to the rest
of your body.

From your spinal cord, smaller
bundles of nerves stretch out like
the branches of a tree. Even smaller
bundles go out to every part of your
body.

Your Five Senses Tell You About the World

All by itself, inside your head, your brain cannot find out what is happening outside you.

Your brain cannot see a bird in a tree. It cannot hear a rock song on the radio. It cannot feel the soft fur of a cat.

Your brain needs your eyes, ears, nose, tongue, and skin. These are your sense organs. They act as lookouts for your brain. They take in information from the world and send nerve messages to your brain.

YOUR FIVE SENSES

Eyes for seeing
Light enters your eyes. Nerves carry messages to the seeing center of your brain.

Ears for hearing
Sound waves in the air enter your ears. Nerves carry messages to the hearing center of your brain.

Nose for smelling
Smells in the air enter your nose. Nerves send messages to the smelling center of your brain.

Tongue for tasting
Taste buds on your tongue send nerve messages to your brain about the taste of your food.

Skin for touching
Nerves in your skin tell your brain whether something is smooth or rough, hot or cold, hard or soft.

Look at all that's inside you—muscles and bones, stomach and intestines, lungs and heart and blood vessels, brain and nerves. Everything works together so you can do the things you like to do.

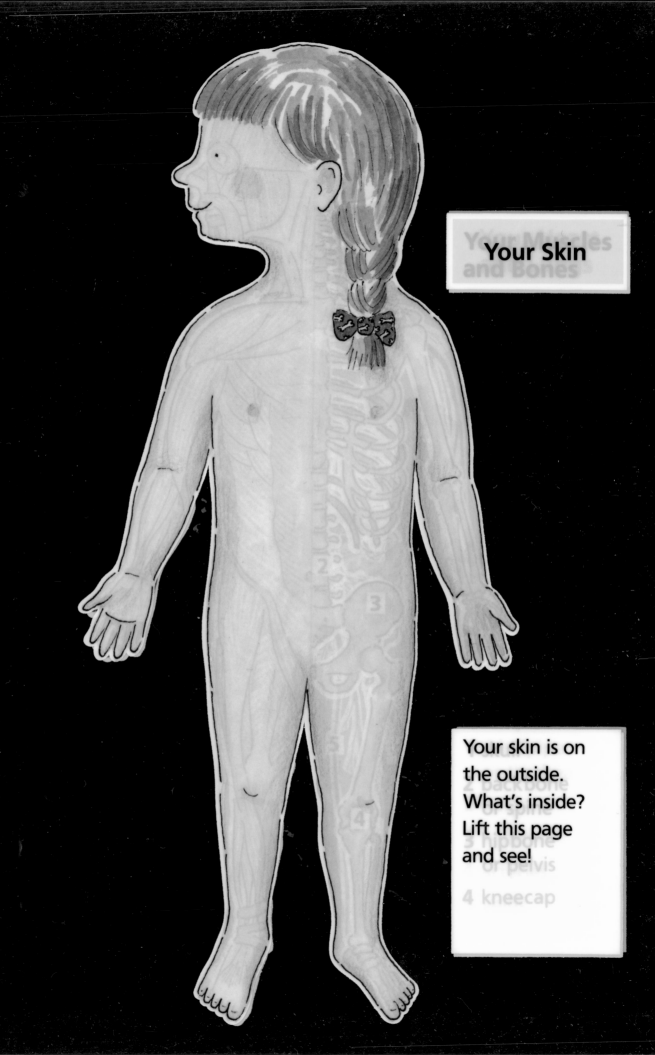

Your Muscles
and Bones

Your Skin

Your skin is on
the outside.
What's inside?
Lift this page
and see!

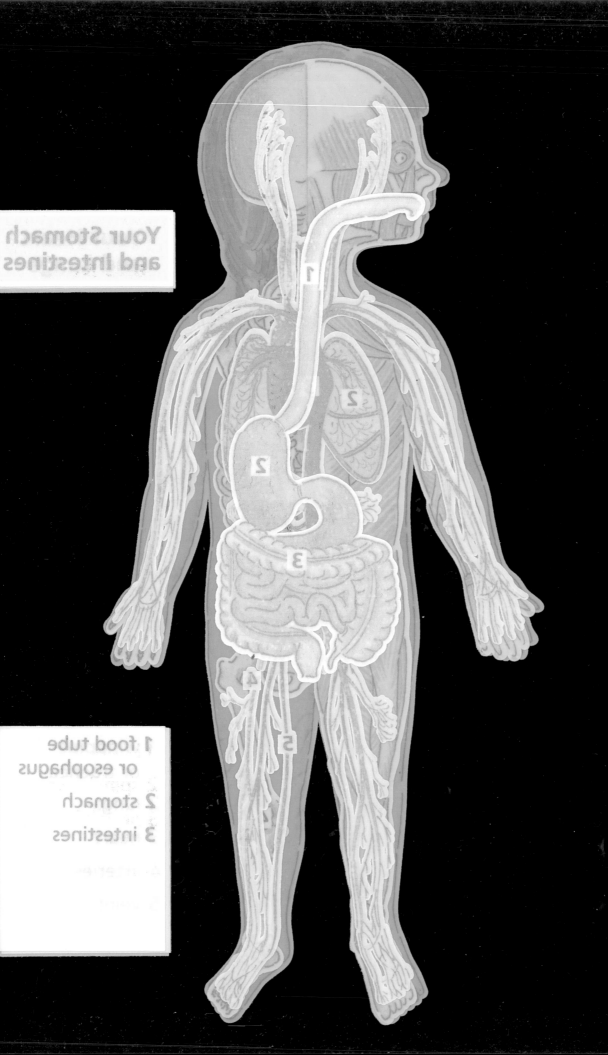

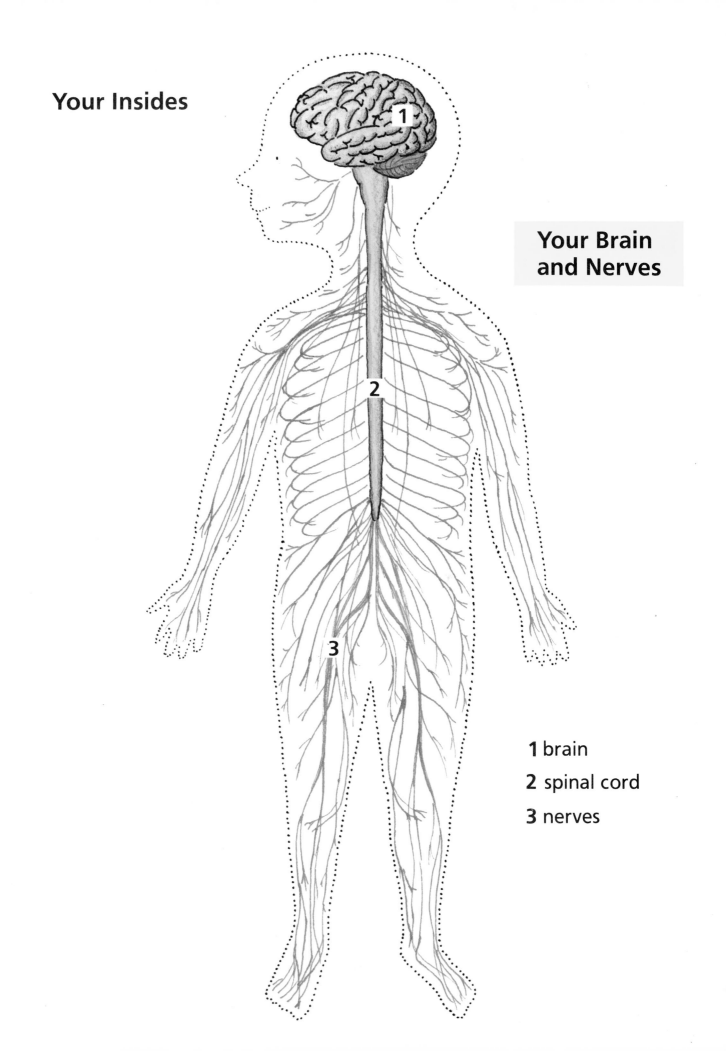

Your Insides

Your Brain and Nerves

1 brain
2 spinal cord
3 nerves

Your Wonderful Skin

Every inch of you has a special covering—your skin. It keeps everything inside *in*, and it keeps dirt and germs *out*.

Your skin takes care of you another way, too. When you get hot, your skin lets out a salty liquid called sweat. Air dries the sweat and cools you off.

Your skin has pores
Did you know that your skin has tiny holes called "pores"? Sweat comes out of these pores. Oil comes out, too. It keeps your skin soft and smooth.

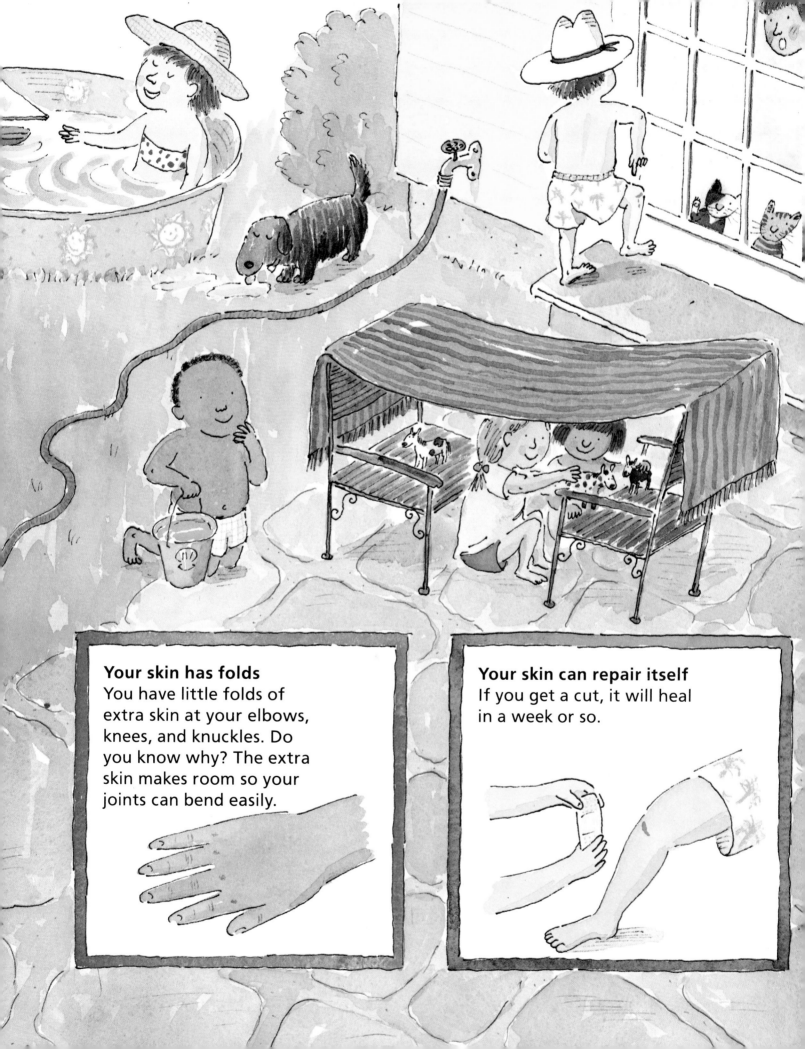

Your skin has folds
You have little folds of extra skin at your elbows, knees, and knuckles. Do you know why? The extra skin makes room so your joints can bend easily.

Your skin can repair itself
If you get a cut, it will heal in a week or so.

Now you've seen your insides *and*
your outsides. Aren't you amazing?